THE

RAISING TEENAGERS

BY SALLY FRANZ
ILLUSTRATED BY STEVE MOLLOY

Nightingale Press

an imprint of Wimbledon Publishing Company Ltd.

LONDON

First published in Great Britain
by Wimbledon Publishing Co. Ltd
London P.O. Box 9779 SW19 7ZG

ISBN: 1 903222 40 0

Produced in Great Britain
Printed and bound in Hungary

BABY BOOMERS

Baby Boomers are everywhere. In the beginning they filled some seventy million baby strollers, then millions of dance halls doing the Lindy Hop and the Twist. At college they filled millions of administration buildings, usually in protest about how hard their life had been this far. Let's face it, they're probably the biggest group of babies the world has ever known. I should know, I'm one of them!

...And whingers. We have taken complaining to a new level. My parents were middle class, so, of course, I had to denounce them as capitalist pigs (right after they paid for my clothes, car and tuition).

I grew up under a government which guaranteed

civil liberties and freedom of speech, so I used my freedom to drop out and criticize.

Inevitably, the fire of youth gradually burned out and, somewhere along the way, my life of dissolution turned into management, mortgages and materialism.

But then something even more horrible happened - I turned forty and became part of the *older generation*.

Dealing with the horror of becoming my own parents hasn't been easy. But Baby Boomers are good at re-inventing themselves. In fact, we invented the term 're-inventing yourself'!

Now we are having to admit to ourselves that

we might just be able to trust someone over thirty, or forty or fifty or, God help us, sixty! And as these rules change we find that life goes on. Though not without a few more obstacles to overcome…

So with all the enthusiasm of hurling oneself in protest over a police barrier, we strike out to the new frontiers of life as mature (or at least wrinkled) Baby Boomers.

INTRODUCTION TO RAISING TEENAGERS

Once a sweet, innocent child, full of laughter and curiosity, hanging onto your every word in awe ... now your offspring has metamorphosed into a different creature. Suddenly gripped by rampant hormones, your 'baby' now makes *The Exorcist* seem like an accurate fly-on-the-wall family documentary. Gone are the days of fairy stories at bed-time, now it's just one long nightmare!

Their once happy laughter has turned into

snickering and low-level sarcasm. Curiosity has been replaced with boredom, deep sighs and eye-rolling. Charm has given way to moods so dark they'd scare Dracula back from the dead. They are surly, uncooperative, selfish, mean-spirited and destructive. And that's not the least of it!

It gets worse - they come in packs, devour all edible matter in a house in less than five minutes and refuse to engage in rational conversation.

Raising teenagers is like trying to negotiate with goldfish. They expect you to feed them, clean up after them and appreciate them for no other reason than the fact they exist.

So why do we put up with them? Well, first of all we already have so much invested in them: education, holiday camp, braces ... and in some countries they can lead to tax deductions. Also, we hope that after they get through this little nasty patch they will become decent human beings. There remains a slight sense of responsibility, we *did* bring them into the world, after all. But this obligation is severely tested as they write off the family car, punk their hair, skip school, have sex in your house and lie to your face about drug use.

They are a crafty lot, but they are also the next generation - the generation that will take care of you as you enter your twilight years. It would probably be a good idea to try to stay on their best side to avoid an early euthanasia.

IDENTIFYING
THE SPECIES

THE 'STUD'

He likes to show he is a man. He has earrings,
a nose ring and a tongue bar. He can take pain, he
can take jeers, he can take discomfort. What he
can't take is a trip abroad, because airport
security won't let him past the metal detectors.

THE INDIVIDUAL

She has barbed wire around her waist, a skull and cross bones on her chest, a black widow spider on her cheek. This she does to become more of an 'enigma'. As she put it, aged sixteen, "I want to be different, just like all my friends."

THE GOTH

He only wears black - from dyed hair to metal-capped boots. He wears black eye make-up and nail polish. Dracula, death and doom cover his walls. It's like sharing a house with the living dead. He feels his parents don't understand him - small wonder when he looks like a mortician in drag.

THE STABLEGIRL

She spends hour upon hour grooming … her
horse's mane. Too bad she doesn't spend
a bit more time on her own looks. While Black
Beauty is all braided and wearing fine leather, the
stablegirl looks as though she's been sleeping
under the hay. Her parents can't wait to send
Beauty off to the show, but try not to show off
their daughter at all.

THE JOCK

He has made good use of his desk at school
... as a counter for his sports trophies. Soccer,
basketball, wrestling, tennis, swimming, golf -
anything that takes him away from studying!
How can he get into college? No problem - he
has a full sports scholarship. And as long as he
doesn't open his mouth in class they won't know
he can't read.

THE SORCEROR

He is in the White Wizard's chambers with a
dagger, a magical cape and a dragon: too bad they
can't help him do his algebra homework. He has a
secret code ring: too bad it doesn't stop him
stuttering when he talks to girls. His parents think
he's upstairs studying. They are obviously under
some kind of enchantment spell.

.

THE HACKER

He learned how to turn on a computer before
he spoke his first word. At thirteen he still isn't
what you'd call verbal. He has cracked into
every nook and cranny of the cyber world: big
business accounts and government files. His folks
drive about with a proud bumper sticker on their
car: 'IBM Young Programmer of the Year' ... just
above the concealed CIA bug on the back
windscreen wiper.

THE ENTREPRENEUR

He was trading lunch money for quiz answers
before he was in first grade. He invested the
money in exam papers and chocolate chip
cookies, which he sells at break-time. But he has a
soft spot: he lends money to his mother at only
15% interest.

MALL RAT

She spends all day shopping. She likes shoes and make-up A LOT! She has big hair, 2 inch nails that spell 'I Rule', and a rhinestone necklace that spells - BRAT! She also has Daddy's charge card. Good thing her parents are divorced and she can play the guilt game for goodies.

THE ECO-WARRIOR

She thinks the world should be dressed in hessian and eat tofu pie. She plaits her hair, uses aloe leaves to cleanse her skin and rides her bicycle instead of driving. She considers her parents 'fossil fuel' - grassland gluttons. She is totally natural and lives off the earth - well, except for hot showers, refrigerated food, clean clothes, CDs…

THE DISPOSAL UNIT

Old Mother Hubbard went to the cupboard
and when she got there the cupboard was bare.
No doubt she had teenagers. This one can
consume a loading dock worth of cookies and a
ship tanker worth of juice as a snack to hold off
until dinner. Come 7pm, there'd better be enough
food to feed a small country, or the family dog
could end up in the oven.

THE TELEPHONIST

She loves to talk. In fact, she can gas for six hours straight about a two hour shopping spree she had with her best friend. She is on the phone describing what she bought now. Who is she telling? Her best friend, of course. What *are* you talking about? "Stuff. You wouldn't understand!" (She's right about that!)

THE DESTROYER

He is a great big puppy dog. Last year he was just
a child; this year he's a child with size thirteen
shoes and hands like shovels. He collides into
everything, knocks over the lamps, the tables and
chairs. He breaks the beds, doors, and the
dressers. Imagine the damage to your roof tiles
when he finally grows into his feet.

THE ROCKER

He wanted to become a rock star. He punked his hair to look like a rooster. He had pins in his nose, studs in his mouth and stars in his eyes. He wore big black boots. Then he tried something different with his music: he stopped taking lessons and bought bigger speakers. He was an overnight success.

THE HIPPIE

Knee-deep in tarot cards, feng shui and grass tea, her job in life is to reach a higher plane of consciousness. This of course does not include saving her allowance, cleaning her room and other earthly burdens.

THE ANGEL

When all her friends are anti-social, she is
charming and delightful. Always respectful of
adults. Never rebelling against authority.
Her term paper was titled, 'How love can
change the world'. She is having an affair
with her father's best friend.

THE NET SURFER

The saying goes, 'When God closes a door he opens a window'. When your teens close *their* doors they're opening up Windows. And the only view you're likely to get for the next six hours is the back of their heads. What are they doing that's so engrossing? They go shopping in virtual malls, visit chat rooms and have pretend conversations with pretend people. If you should happen to suggest that they go outside for some fresh air, what's the reply? "Oh mum, GET REAL!"

THE PLAYBOY

There comes a day when a boy realizes he wants
to touch a girl in a way other than tackling her in
the mud and making her cry. But our playboy
can't be bothered with the next phase of kissing
and dating. He prefers to fantasize a more
thrilling romance ... with a little help from the
educational material beneath his mattress. He has
'studied' hard to find out what women want -
especially the ones in the magazines. Of course
he never tests the theory out in the real world -
he doesn't have time, he's too busy 'reading'.

CALL OF THE WILD
TEENAGER

I'm bored, there's nothing
to do around here.

(Said as he rests his feet on the
basket of clean, unfolded laundry.)

I hate you.

(Said just after receiving an allowance for
doing nothing more than breathing.)

I wish I had never
been born.

(This from the premature baby who cost
a fortune in medical bills and took
thirty six hours in labour.)

You've ruined my life.

(Heard just as you get a postcard from a single
friend vacationing in Barbados.)

If you buy me a car
I will never speed.

(Delivered with a straight face, forgetting that
you were once a teenager as well.)

I hate living in this house.

(Uttered moments after picking out
new wallpaper for her own room.)

You're not cool.

(From the child with a nose ring,
green hair and untied shoes.)

Bobby and I are in love!
We want to get married.
We aren't going to make
the kind of mistakes
you and Dad made.

(Said blowing big pink bubblegum
bubbles in your face.)

I already did my homework.

(True, if one was to think of homework
as a once in a lifetime event.)

Everybody else's parents
are letting them go.

(That is, all those parents who are doing time for
robbery, car theft and embezzlement.)

I'm hungry, isn't there anything good to eat?

(Said after inhaling the entire pantry, crumbs and wrappers.)

Nothing.

(After asking what they did all day. Probably the truth.)

Can it wait? I'm busy.

(Now of course after doing nothing all day
they are busy watching TV and can't help
with dinner ... except for the eating part.)

How dare you go through
my things and invade
my privacy!

(Said after being caught with weed
and a bong in his room.)

Buy me a puppy,
I promise I'll walk it.

(The next day she walks right past the dog
and drives away with her friends.)

You don't trust me!

(Spoken by the teen who has been caught
shoplifting, smoking, drinking and never
comes home before 2am.)

I hate skiing/horse-riding/sailing. I only do it because you want me to.

(Said after a small fortune has been spent on equipment and clothes at their request.)

When I grow up I will never ever be like you!

(Didn't you say this to your parents and now look!)

AUNT SASSY'S ADVICE COLUMN

Advice to help parents and teenagers deal with
the years between 'puberty and probity'.

Dear Aunt Sassy,

I am very popular. I have a lot of friends and things to do. But get this - my parents expect me to be home for dinner every night.
How uncool is that?

Popular in Peterborough

Dear Ms. Popular,

I know it seems unreasonable that your folks want you back at home by the end of the day. It is probably a throw-back to ancient times when young girls found on the streets after dark were eaten by lions.

I am sure if you came up with a good reason why you should be out until the small hours they would oblige. Perhaps if you were spending all that valuable time doing something worthwhile such as founding a new charity or researching a cure for cancer rather than drinking your way into oblivion?

Unselfishly yours,

AUNT SASSY

Dear Aunt Sassy,

My parents grounded me just because I had a few friends over when they were away. Is that fair?

Manacled in Macclesfield

Dear Manacled,

Not much is fair about the modern world. Parents are tediously protective of the meagre belongings that they have been able to scrape together while keeping you in shoes, food and school. I am sure it was only a small gouge in only one of the matching glass end tables and that black permanent marker stain on the beige carpet is hardly noticeable if the lights are off.

I suppose you could have asked them beforehand but they would probably have said "NO".

I can't think why.

Protectively yours,

AUNT SASSY

Dear Pressured,

This is a cruel world. Yes, people actually expect you to do something in exchange for money. Not like your parents who have let you freeload for eighteen years.

Given your experience to date perhaps you could get a job as a tester for new types of beer or video games. People who do this kind of work are called 'focus group members'. The operative word here is 'focus' - are you with me? Focus. Concentration. Over here, Mr. Preston! That's a good boy.

Attentively yours,

AUNT SASSY

Dear Aunt Sassy,

Ever since my child reached twelve years old she has acted like a different person. Should I be concerned that she has a personality disorder?

Fearful in Frankfurt

Dear Fearful,

The onset of the teenage years brings with it overwhelming adult responsibility and a tidal wave of hormones. Your child, as one father put it, is going down 'into the tunnel'. She will emerge a charming loving adult - in about eight years. Until then prepare for each meal to have the warmth of a an Arab-Israeli summit.

It's a bit like being a lion tamer - while the lion can bite your head off, you still have to train it, feed it and pick up after it. If it's any consolation, you still own the circus.

Stalemates and debates,

AUNT SASSY

Dear Aunt Sassy,

My parents are so uncool. They won't let me have a motorcycle, or hang out late at night, or spend the weekend with my girlfriend camping.
Talk to them!

Bummed out in Boston

Dear Bummed,

Okay let's review the number one law of safety: 'No one is safe in an unsafe place!' Unsafe places include: the fast lane while on a motorcycle between a forty ton truck and a delivery van; bad neighbourhoods after hours where all the people in the street are armed and drunk; and any teenage boy alone with any teenage girl at any time.

Perhaps you had intended to drive an antique motorcycle around a slow track, or were going to an all-night prayer meeting. Perhaps you were camping with your girlfriend and her seven foot tall wrestler brother. If so I apologize, profusely. But I'd bet my support hose the answer to these is NOT!

Safe and sound,

AUNT SASSY

GUIDELINES FOR DEALING WITH TEENAGERS

The guidelines for raising and surviving teenagers are complex and arduous (why would anything dealing with teenagers be easy?). But cheer up. They will out-grow this awkward phase, just not before they've turned every hair on your head grey (those hairs, that is, that you haven't already torn out). Good luck!

■   *If you want them to avoid unwanted pregnancy (is there any other kind for children under eighteen?) let them babysit for families with five children all under the age of six for several days at a time. One family I know has three teenage girls of babysitting age. They are all going into the convent immediately after graduation.*

■ *If you haven't talked about sex before, you must do it now (tell them, that is). But remember, try not to extol the joys of sex - they really aren't mature enough to experiment. Beware of telling them that sex is bad, because, well, there's no need for them to know about YOUR sex life, is there?*

■ *If they want to date, insist they talk on the phone for two hours to their 'special friend' every night for an entire month before the first date. Most teen relationships are over in the first three weeks so they will never end up in each other's arms. Better yet, let them cyberdate, that way they can pretend they are in a relationship (computer viruses are less life-threatening than anything they could catch on a real date!).*

■ *Encourage sports. Why? Because most coaches*
are sadistic and will wear them out. Very few
teenagers want to party when they have just
completed their 100th lap around the track. Even if
they don't make the team, tell them to go to practice
to prove how tough they are.

■ *Running a household with teenagers is not a democracy. It's more like a mutual hostile take-over. Therefore you do not have to 'trust them'. You do not have to 'be fair' and you do not have to believe them when they say "everybody else is doing it". This is war! Albeit, civil war.*

■ *Punishment is not supposed to be a day at the country club. But, time and again, parents confine their children to the very place where there is TV, food and entertainment - home sweet home. No, dear parents, real punishment should be grown-up punishment. Make them go to work with you. Beware they're not better at your job than you!*

■   *If your teenager has just constructed a life-size model of the Eiffel Tower in the backyard with empty beer cans, he or she might be drinking too much. Likewise if he or she has obtained a nickname from their peers such as 'Tanked', 'Trashed' or 'Wasted' you might want to run a blood alcohol check before they borrow your new car for a 'road trip'!*

■ *Never let a teenager near a bathroom if you will need it in the next five hours. The amount of time they will take is always in direct proportion to the importance of the meeting you will miss. They can spend thirty minutes doing their hair and still look like a Rastafarian on a bad hair day.*

■ *And remember, 'Your children don't 'make you mad' they 'reveal your character."*

CONCLUSION

Teenagers are God's way of keeping you humble and broke. A homeless man approached me and asked for spare change - I told him, "I have teenagers, there was a shake-down before I even left the house." He replied - "How do you think I became homeless?!"

Teens are attacked by hormones, caught in an identity crisis and terrified about the prospects of having to find a career. It will not help the situation to tell them these are the best years of their lives. It will not reassure them to know the awful truth that hormones, identity crises and career issues only get worse as you get older.

And it will not help to tell them that you were once a teenager yourself - even the vaguest mental picture of you passionately kissing in the back of a car will cause them to vomit.

What can you do? You can wait. You can fix a lock and rig an alarm system to the drinks cabinet, the fridge freezer, and your car. You can give them a pager and try to keep in contact, or better yet a tracking device so you can follow them via satellite.

Trying to cut your losses? Perhaps you can turn your house into an old-fashioned coin-operated arcade. Want clean clothes? Deposit your change in the slot. Food? Coins! Milk? Coins! Car? Stop by the petrol station on your way out. Telephone? Definitely coin-operated. Stereo? One pound for each turn of the volume. If they want to destroy their ear drums you should at least get reimbursed for your hearing loss.

Finally, remember that somewhere, deep under all that attitude and disregard for the rest of the family, there is still a small child, being held captive by rampant hormones. One day it will be set free. It *will* be worth the wait.

This might be a good time to ask your parents how they managed to survive you!